Crash!

by Dean DeRamus

illustrated by Marilyn Janovitz

Grace and Mitch raced around the rug.

"Grace, what broke?" Mitch asked.

Grace gulped and moved to the side.

Mitch asked, "What was that?"

"It was Mom's white rose vase,"

Grace said.

"Gramps," the kids yelled, "help us!"

"What is it?" Gramps asked.

Mitch and Grace picked up the vase.

"Well, we have a big mess to fix,"

Gramps said.

The big clock chimed five times.

"Mom and Dad will be home at ten,"

Grace said. "Can we fix it in time?"

Gramps fixed the rose vase.

Then he glanced at the clock.

"We did it," he yelled.

"Gramps is the best," Grace and

Mitch yelled.

6

Mom and Dad came in.

"Did you have fun with Gramps?"
Mom asked.

"Yes, Gramps fixed the rose vase,"
Mitch said.

"Gramps fixed the rose vase?" Mom asked. Mitch handed Mom the rose vase. "Do not run around the rug," Gramps said.

Mitch and Grace smiled.